Gesture

Gesture

NANCY JAKOBSSON

iUniverse, Inc.
Bloomington

Gesture

iUniverse books may be ordered through booksellers or by contacting:

iUniverse
1663 Liberty Drive
Bloomington, IN 47403
www.iuniverse.com
1-800-Authors (1-800-288-4677)

ISBN: 978-1-4620-3105-4 (sc)
ISBN: 978-1-4620-3106-1 (ebk)

Printed in the United States of America

iUniverse rev. date: 07/26/2011

For those who have shared their stories with me and those who have shared in mine.

Gesture
Every object, every person has a natural gesture or line of movement that is individual and specific. In drawing, one hopes to capture the essence of that line, give life to the subject.

Notes from a drawing class with Doug Erion

Special thank you to Veronica Patterson, inspiring teacher, gentle guide and supportive friend.

"Instructions for living a life:
Pay attention.
Be astonished.
Tell about it."

Mary Oliver, *Sometimes*

CONTENTS

I

The Cold

First Sonnet

I've come to know the light before light,

a gray ghost that walks on soft feet

pulling morning in from the night.

Slowly the darkness retreats.

I love to wake in that hour of gray,

lie watching the shadows move on the wall,

keep watch until they all fade away.

My fleeting dreams I attempt to recall

as daylight slides in beneath the shade.

The slow boat of morning arrives at my door.

Each day the same plan is played.

Nothing as certain, nothing so sure-

the best part of the day lasts until noon.

I depend on morning, like I count on the moon.

Nancy Jakobsson

This Is the Cold

This is the cold I measure
all other cold against
Chicago in January
wind off the lake
waiting for the bus.

It pierces layers of clothing,
penetrates bones
It's deep blue,
takes hours to bleed out,
lingers in the coat closet.

It's dusk, not defined by light or sky,
but by time
half hour from the Loop
half hour bus ride
home by dark.

Fullerton Avenue, beneath the L tracks,
the rumble of the northbound train rises
from the dark like a giant eel,
winds beneath the streets of the city.
A rush of speed from the tunnel
trails a screech of metal on metal.

I've just missed the #40 bus
and wait. Inside the waiting
I calculate the hours waiting
for buses and subways
since my father's death
my mother's refusal to drive.

I notice the crusty black snow
piled high against steel posts.
Once white, then gray
becomes a dark sludge
that covers the streets,
now more soot than snow.

On that night in late January
I board the #40 bus, knowing
I will leave
the cold, the gloom,
no room for sky.

Listen Well

Listen with the ear beneath the ear
to the story under the story,
the dark before the dark,
the hurt behind the hurt.

Listen with the ear inside the ear,
wait for the word that catches in the throat,
follow the pause that opens to the unsayable,
a story that begins and ends in the same place,
a deep well that sustains or poisons.

Listen as you would feel
for a breeze in the dark,
intent on not missing the direction or flow.
close both eyes
to see with the other eye

Listen well.
Hold the tongue under the tongue.

The Cat Has Her Way

Sitting in the blue chair by the bedroom window

journal open on my lap, pen poised

to write about the morning.

The way the rain is falling,

each drop heavy with night.

How it soaks the spread of leaves

beneath the linden tree.

The way the weight of sleep

lingers across my shoulders

like an old sweater.

I want to describe the exact way

light breaks beneath the shade.

I'm ready to fill the blank page

with all the eloquence I can muster.

Now my gray cat forces herself

between pen and page,

fills my lap with her weight

and the moment.

Wrightwood Avenue

I remember the red brick apartment building
on Wrightwood Avenue where I lived
with my mother and father.

I remember my father, always reading,
a cigarette burning in the copper ashtray,
the round table piled with books and newspapers.
I would stand behind him, playing barber,
comb his hair that feels like mine, thick and coarse.

I remember my mother
changing my father's dressing
after the cancer surgery.
They were in the bathroom, the door half open.
She uncovered the red incision,
stitches like thin black wire.
She wound white gauze around his neck
like a scarf.
I watched. My father saw me,
and said nothing.

I remember the gang of kids that lived in our building .
We would play in the backyard, in the alley,
on the back porches, in the basement when it rained,
but never in each other's apartments.

I remember the day my mother came home from the hospital.
buying a dress for my father's funeral
the American flag on his casket
the way his face looked
lips pressed, cheeks too red
the smell of carnations
riding in a black limousine
with my mother and aunt
coming home and my friends not asking
and me not telling.

Then it was August.
I had my twelfth birthday
my mother bought twin beds
school started
and I was in the seventh grade.

Nancy Jakobsson

Waiting for the Tea to Simmer on a Cold Autumn Morning Before Leaving on a Long Journey

The iron teapot on the stove
is the color of the morning sky.
The yellow-orange flame
like the sun which sleeps
below the horizon.
The air is cold
and I am full of dread
for today I must travel far
with no companion at my side.
My cup now empty,
I must leave, for nothing
comes from the map or
the tea leaves. No direction
what so ever.

What If

he had not been the youngest of fourteen children,
destined to leave the island, no more than a boy,
to follow his older brother to America.

What if that new country had not gone to war,
and he had not been asked to serve
a country not yet his.

What if he had died in that war
and not returned to his homeland
to marry the woman he loved.

What if she had not waited.

What if they had not moved to Chicago
to find work, he was a carpenter,
carpenters always found work.

What if the Depression hadn't come
and there was no work
and the woman moved back to their homeland
with their baby, to live with her parents

and the man sold everything they had,

just to get by.

What if years later,

when the woman returned

and things were good,

their only child had not a brain tumor.

She was only ten when they operated

and she died anyway.

If Margaret hadn't died,

would my parents have conceived

another child?

Litany of Color

Let there be bright yellow
somewhere in the middle of my life,
a place to come when it's dark inside.
Let there be a sharp angle of red
that cuts through like danger or fear
or the unplanned, a color I seldom wear.
Let there be wisps of blue and green,
grasses and seaweed that gentle
my way of seeing through things.
Let purple sudden into wonder.
Let it swirl in and out of everything
that's important or lasts.
Touch blue, purple, red, green.
Fingerprints petal into flowers
in unexpected places.
Most of all let my hands be covered
with patterns-smudged
by touching, touching.

Progress Notes

On first meeting
She carried her grief like a boulder.
The weight of it formed her center
rounding her shoulders.

In her eyes the haze she walks through.
The chair's edge
balances go or stay.

She tells her story
stepping from stone to stone
across a swollen river.

Months later
On this warm summer day
she wears layers of shirts
over her uncertainties.

Scratches on her hands, evidence
of anxious picking at
small pains.
Another session

She sorts through the fray of papers
at loose ends in her spiral notebook
memory scraps held together
with anger, tears and regret
unfolding from the past.

Today
I see her face for the first time,
her hair tucked back
with a red scarf.

Her large purple poncho
swirls with intention.
She begins talking
before I ask a question.

Horses Lost and Found

The horses returned to the field by my house today,

back from their summer home in the mountains.

Like the first frost and shorter days,

their presence foretells winter.

In the perfect low light of late afternoon

they pose in groups of two or three,

in a wash of green and gold,

still as statues of themselves.

Most absorbed in grazing, heads bowed,

solid and sure as grace and forgiveness.

A black and smaller gray

stand side by side, head to head,

only that.

As a child I collected small plastic horses,

kept them in a box under my bed,

gave them names only I knew,

created my idea of horse,

arranging them on the landscape

of floor and kitchen table.

I wonder what became of them,

the blacks, the browns, a single white, a palomino.

Lost with a favorite doll and books, innocence, a father.

I stop at the field in the early morning

and at the quiet end of day.

Someday these horses will go-

give way to streets and houses.

But not today-not this season.

They'll stay through the winter.

II

What Is

A Conversation.

Why solitude?
The sky answers with a resounding yes.

And longing, what's the purpose of longing?
The wind repeats its answer again and again.

Ask trees the question of grace.

Why such stillness?
The snow is silent.

Tell me about balance.
Light and shadow over the landscape.

And what about God?

Receiving the News

It begins with no.
~erupts and takes you
to your knees,
demanding, ranting, grasping.
~becomes two syllables:
the long O, round and hollow
fills the room, sucks out the air.

Walls and windows shudder. No
~breaks out, spreads
across dark landscape,
~falls into empty streets.

Each no
~echoes into the night,
~comes up every morning
~ repeats and repeats, slowly
fills an emptied life.

Then one day, no
~hardens into
a small silent stone of is.

Sunday Visits

How when I was driving there I'd say
I'd stay for at least an hour.

How I'd climb the stairs to her second floor apartment.

How I would engage and elicit.

How she would withdraw and escape.

We pulled that rope between us.

How she'd come to wear the same green dress,
two sizes too large, food stains on the front.

How I'd try not to notice.

How her furniture was worn smooth. How
the refrigerator shelves were mostly empty. How
she'd canceled the paper again.

How life was a story she'd read and forgotten.

How death had stolen her reason for being,
mother, wife. How

we knew I was all she had left.

Let There Be Birds

Their condition asks if it is time to be.

Thomas Merton

There on the horizon,
over the foothills,
tiny dots
like seeds scattered
across the morning sky.

Now overhead
like a cloud of insects.
black birds,
wave after wave
in random flight.
A chorus of chirps and snaps.

Ahead
more birds
in the tops of trees.
They seem to cheer
those in flight.

The trees and sky alive with birds.

Then at an appointed time
with the downbeat

of an invisible hand,
they too lift off.
A blanket of birds
fluffs from the trees
sweeps in a wide arc
after the others.

At once, it's still.
Sunrise paints
the tops of trees
with yellow light.
Across the river
on long-fingered branches
two cormorants
watch.

Nancy Jakobsson

As I Have

For my father, Sven Johan Nesheim

What do I know of this man
who spent his nights reading,
papers and books scattered
around his chair.
He would carefully put on his glasses,
snap the hard black case,
shut the world around him.
Or of the man in the photograph
kneeling next to his young daughter,
one arm resting on his knee
his straight-ahead smile
repeated in my son's steady grin.
How much time can I capture
from his gold pocket watch
worn smooth by touchBhis and mine,
from a walk for the newspaper
when I was seven or eight.
I tried to match his stride,
his one to my two.
How mother would say, years later

I walked like my dad.

How I longed to say

father,

hold the word on my tongue,

savor the sound-rub it smooth.

Now, at an age

he never knew,

I wonder about his dying.

Did he weep or rage,

plead for more?

Nancy Jakobsson

Grays Asks Nothing

new from dark.
The morning
breathes out,
lifts night
from the eastern sky,
reveals the day
in shades of gray.

The lake
a flat sheet.
A solitary duck
breaks the surface
its black silhouette
trailing long
thin lines.

Grass and willows
define the shore.
The trees behind:
bare branches
etched into
the sky.

The fog lifts
from the water's face
exhales haze.
Silence seeps
into the seams
of the day.

Given a Choice

after Wislawa Szymborska

I prefer the moon

I prefer kindness

I prefer gray

I prefer trees leafless

I prefer curiosity

I prefer the ambivalence of cats

I prefer questions

I prefer autumn, which has purpose

I prefer the slant light of late afternoon

I prefer wondering

I prefer wondering about God

I prefer wonder

I prefer the great blue heron in all of his poses

I prefer rivers

I prefer mornings, full of possibilities

I prefer possibilities to expectations

I prefer the truth

I prefer silence to virtually any noise, especially as the
sun rises

I prefer having a choice

Nancy Jakobsson

I'm Glad You Asked

Me? I'm in a funk.

Out of sorts, really.

Nothing seems to fit.

I'm uncomfortable in my own skin,

tired of my feet,

they're too big for my shoes.

Really, I should take a walk,

keep walking north

all the way to the Wyoming.

I don't like Wyoming.

Wind blows all day long.

Makes you crazy, takes

your breath away.

You can't get enough oxygen.

It's more than being irritated.

It's being the source of all irritation,

right in the middle of everything

that's bothersome, nose dripping,

eye watering, itchy, sticky

summer-in-Chicago,

middle-of-August irritated.

I want to take my shoes off,

climb out of my too-tight skin,

scratch my eyes out,

break my grandmother's china,

yell obscenities in two languages,

be all out, in your face, over the top,

outside anybody's too small box,

pissed-off, pissed-on, pissy, PMSy,

sticks and stones and all my bones,

step-on-the-cat's-tail ANGRY.

Nothing to Do

When waiting to hear if a friend has died
there's no good thing to do.
Another friend said she ironed
listening to a sad song,
her hot tears smoothed away.
I can think of nothing to fill
the breath between
knowing and not.
So I sit here and wait, as if waiting
is the thing to do, trying to feel
the scratch of the blue chair's fabric
on my arms.

Moon, Swan

Moon	Swan
slips	glides
own	across
the	the
dark	water
pond	along
a	the
silver	silver
path	light
wakes	becomes
the	the
sleeping	moon's
swan	shadow

Nancy Jakobsson

Intersection

She

northbound on Quebec

He

eastbound on 14th

The officer

not in pursuit

his lights were on

The officer

in pursuit

turned his lights off

The intersection

northbound car

slammed

stacked up

broke

landed

on

He

eighteen

had a felony arrest

thrown from his car

died at the scene

They

tried to extricate

transported to

She

pronounced

The call

came at 10:30

No

stop the eastbound car

stop the northbound car

turn lights on

turn lights off

I can't pronounce dead

Nancy Jakobsson

Casida of the Moon

The moon

was not searching

for a place to rest

in the endless night

it was searching for something else.

Was the moon searching

for the edge of eternity

for the roaring winds of solitude

or for something else.

The moon

was not searching

it was I who was searching

and the moon was the path

to something else.

Room in New York

Edward Hopper, 1932

The room is narrow,
the space between them vast.

She at the upright
alone with her thoughts
picks out a tune
familiar and sad.

He with his paper
open to the financials,
a thin wall of numbers
he retreats behind.

She wears a new red dress
he doesn't notice.

His tie still in place,
tied tight as the knot in his throat.

Neither one speaks

Nancy Jakobsson

as they leave for the evening.

He'll drink too much,
she'll pick a fight.

They'll return to the room,
break open the ripe wound of silence,
unleashing the words.
Then retreat
into silence again.

III

Longest Hours

Questions

He could no longer live inside his life.
He quit teaching, his apartment,
wearing ties, moved to the south side
to a walk-up,
worked in the steel mills, nights,
doing I don't know what.
Wrote poetry, kept loving me,
and I don't know why.

He wanted something
from himself, the world,
his writing, from the man
who asked for spare change
on the street corner, in the city,
near the jazz club, from me.

Questions hung between us
like unopened letters.
So I married a man
whose answers hung on his chest
like medals from a battle
that would be ours to fight.

Nancy Jakobsson

It Was Different This Time

Something usually got broken
a glass
the door
the wall
her will.
The words were the same
words with sharp letters
that left scars.

But this time
the mother said stop,
one son called the police,
the other hid behind the couch.
They couldn't call them back
the words.

The police came.
The father left.

That night
they all slept in the same bed,

on their backs

with their eyes open,

the older boy with his baseball bat.

They waited for headlights,

for pounding on the door.

The mother had silver in her eyes

as if she had swallowed the moon

with the night.

Nancy Jakobsson

When It Took So Long to Build

I should have known
that the cold would pile
deep in the corners,
cover the walls and windows.
I should have known
it would enter my dreams
too much to melt.

Should I have known
when the winds raged
that the walls would never come straight,
and nothing fit the way it was.
Should I have known
there would be no place to hide
from what we couldn't see?

Hearing

He pushes the court room door open;
she follows a few steps back, hoping
he keeps his pace and she can drop
behind. After this many years she has
difficulty reading his body language.
Is it defeat, depression, indifference
that she sees? What becomes of rage
when it burns itself out? One thing
certain is her wish to avoid
confrontation or even conversation.
The corridor is vacant; theirs is the first
hearing of the day. The walls are pale
gray, the wood floor worn and her
sweater beige. As if lit by 40 watt bulbs,
no color interprets the day.

Nancy Jakobsson

Longest Hours

The darkest hour, the waiting

hour, the hour between sleep and dawn.

The hour of regret, which repeats itself.

The hour before, which is twice as long.

The hour that dissolves.

The hourglass half full, half empty.

The first hour holds no time.

The final hour has no weight.

The darkest hour, the waiting.

Words Hold Her

She spins around until

she falls into parts of herself,

loses her name,

nothing to do but

put her together with words,

words so small they can't be read

unless you come very close.

Words hold her together,

all parts of herself.

Words are her eyes,

life, lips.

Come close and read the words-

accept no one's definition-

that form her heart.

Nancy Jakobsson

She Carried a Stone

She carried a stone
in the middle of her life
somewhere in her chest

close to her heart,
formed from the seed of grief,
layer on layer.

It had turned her life
from what she wished
to what would never be.

I was to inherit the stone,
carry it with me.
I took instead the seed.

IV

Grief: An Interlude

Grief Circle

Light fell a certain way that afternoon
as it filtered through the window panes,
forming shadows on the worn wood
floor of the log building. It was
a light seen often at dusk or dawn,
when clocks are quiet. Eight
women sit in a circle on hard
wooden benches pulled close to the
fire which closes the circle.
They-mothers, daughters, lovers,
wives-now mourners drawn
together by their grief. They've
come to tell their stories. As each
speaks time seems to hold out
silence. One waits, choosing to be
last. Cheeks flushed, eyes glazed
with tears, she tells how she and
her son shared her husband's last
hours. Her breathing shallow and
slow, she fears a deeper breath
might reach that place

Nancy Jakobsson

where pain lives. Outside the circle
the room chills; the mountain peaks
hold season's first snow. The fire
and the sound of wind in leaves fill
silence.

I Listen to Stories

The stories we tell have a way of taking care of us.
                                    Barry Lopez

It was the day before Sharon's twenty-sixth birthday, a
Tuesday night, November, when the police came to her
door about her mother's accident.

Mary answered the phone at 1:15 a.m. to hear the news
of her husband's death.

Ben sat by his partner's bed through the night, watching
life seep out of the frail body like sand from a half-empty
sack.

Drew found her husband's body when she awoke, beside
the couch
in their family room, bailing twine around his neck.

They begin at the end and, like a book left open, move
back and forth.

Sharon remembers that the lightbulb in the hallway to her apartment was burned out. She thought the police came because of the loud party the night before.

Ben remembers the sun through the blinds in the hospice center that morning, squares of light crossing the blankets and Bill's face. His light-colored eyelashes gold, fluttering in morphined sleep.

Mary can repeat the conversation with her husband that night on the phone, every word he said, she said, the way he paused just before hanging up: "I love you."

Drew found a pair of scissors next to her husband's body.

I listen for a place in the story where the balance shifts, slightly or suddenly. A place in the story that can open.

~~~

Ben came out to the team he had worked with for two years. He guessed that they knew, but was surprised that they hugged him.

Sharon decided to go to the court hearing for the young man whose blood alcohol level was 2.05 on the night his truck struck her mother's car. She needed to know if she could forgive him.

Mary went to the accident scene today, less than three miles from her house. There was a tree near where he had been hit. "I planted bulbs in the dirt around that tree, hyacinths and daffodils. John loved daffodils. I got down on my hands and knees, traffic going by. I didn't care what people thought."

Drew put the scissors in the box with Pete's ashes. "I've decided to apply for graduate school 40 years later. Why not? I have nothing to lose, nothing else to lose."

Instructions for a New Grief Counselor

First appointment, begin with *When*
did your (husband, mother,
son, sister, friend, etc.) die?
Ask more. Probe further. *What*

was the cause of death?
Reach deep into the ache. *Were you*
with him when he died?
Record the response.

Begin to manipulate the broken ends
This may hurt a bit.
of lives pulled apart, without warning,
or over months, years. *Tell me*
about your pain. Don't disclose
the pieces never fit back into place.
Where does it hurt? In slow detail,
extract hopes, dreams, and memories.

Diagnosis: Grief. Rate it
on a scale from one
to intolerable.
Prognosis:

As long as it takes.

V

Before Turning

She Lived

She lived a full life, maybe a good life,

anyway a life she found worth living.

She lived much of it alone, both early and late.

She was born in a city longing for sky,

lived in a small town, carried the city inside.

She grew between two cultures

learned to speak their languages,

uncertain about both.

She wasn't proud, or only about two things,

her sons and a vision she dreamed into being.

She had many jobs but her work was loss.

She listened to stories, traveled them like foreign

countries.

She made connections between people and ideas.

In a group she preferred being first or last.

She was preceded by many she loved

and survived by many more

who shared their lives with her.

An Unmarked Path

She answers the door.
I give her an awkward hug,
balancing a quiche in one hand,
geranium in the other.
I have the urge to kiss her forehead
as you would a young child,
her too-open face.

Instead, I pass my hand over
the new growth of hair,
a curve of metal staples on the side
shapes the question I don't ask.
Instead say, "who knew you had such a
shapely head?"

One by one we arrive, with food,
flowers, a bottle of champagne.
We talk openly, name the bastard-
glioblastoma, say grade four.
There is no grade five.

We know how to do this,

grew up in hospice.

say *chemotherapy, course of radiation.*

as if this were a class.

We've talked our way up and down

mountains, single file, in pairs,

always following the marked trail.

No signs mark this trip.

As usual, she takes the lead.

Nancy Jakobsson

The One Whose Name I Held

The one whose name I held
before I held him.
The one long waited for.
The one who arrived on a rainy night
but waited for the sun,
whose cord was cut by his father
and cut again years later.
The long crier with long legs
and deep longings.
The one who gathers friends
and loses things.
The one who has little patience
and large presence.
The one who quits rather than lose.
The world comes easy to him
but doesn't stick.
He who rarely plans ahead
but lives into every day.
The one who breaks things,
himself, he'd like to fix
but doesn't know how.

Son with a quick temper.

Son with a generous temperament.

Son of the mountains.

First son.

Nancy Jakobsson

What Andy Goldsworthy Knows

_Looking, touching, material, place and form
are all inseparable from the resulting work._
                    Andy Goldsworthy

What Andy Goldsworthy knows

is beauty and impermanence

are equals

completing is beginning

yellow flowers can be a pool

and stone flows like blood.

He knows form is everything

and function is elusive.

A castle can be built of sticks

or stones and break in water.

You can depend on the tide

but never the wind.

Fleece is a river,

stone wall, path.

He knows the weight of gravity

and the lightness. I want

to live

what Andy Goldsworthy knows.

64

Second Born

For Kris, upon his marriage

To this woman I give my son, I don't say this out loud but think.

Son who at three cried for days when his big wheel was stolen,
learning the world can be unjust.

Seven-year-old who woke at night and slid into our bed,
without a word.

Ten-year-old who, when he learned we were divorcing, said,
"this is the worst day of my life."

He hated good byes and ran with his tears when his grandmother died.

At thirteen he broke the law to test the limits of his new home
and learned justice could come in a uniform with charity.

At sixteen he carried time back with both hands-broken
then repaired.

Son of direction, son who watched.

Enforcer of order, keeper of peace.
Second born.

Nancy Jakobsson

Walk Before Writing

I take the familiar path to the river.
Under the bridge a muted chorus
then three pigeons whoosh
above my head
startling the dog to bark his objection.

After the bridge the path curves with the river.
Stones along the shore have caps of snow
like a mass of white mushrooms.
I break the path's blanket of white,
the crunch of snow like wood aging.

What the snow steals in color
it gives back in form,
outlines branches, flowers shrubs.
A skitter of tiny tracks
make intricate patterns
in the unbroken white.

Morning still pink at the edges,
the sun paints a wash of color
as it slides behind gray clouds.

Snow falls on my face and hair
soft as a whisper in the dark.

A dip-dip of flight, a chickadee
lands on a small tree ahead.
Repeats her name, chicka-dee-dee-dee.
Stops to test the quiet.

From across the river
in a tumble of trees, movement,
a deer, no three.
One stops, holds before turning.

Nancy Jakobsson

Please Don't Cry

The sound of a man crying and
I come undone.
There ought to be a word
for the way my heart lets down
like a nursing mother her milk.

We tell our sons:
It's ok to cry-no, be a man.
Be sensitive-no, be strong.
Be brave, we teach, be tough.
Don't break.

My grown son calls, in tears,
and his voice breaks-as he breaks
the news that they've broken up.
And his heart is broken.

I want to wipe his tears,
smooth his forehead,
make soup, give medicine,
sleep on the floor next to his bed,
tell him a story, make it better, just
please don't cry.

Get Out of My Dreams

You with the suitcase stuffed
with the emptiness of your life,
too much to carry,
you left it behind.
You, when your hair was dark
and grief hadn't stolen your eyes.

Get out, you building that house
and tearing it down,
the same bricks of anger
mortared with empty promises.
You couldn't build it straight
after the winds blew.

Take that baby
in the small wooden box
by the window.
It's not mine.
Breathe life into its limp body.

All of you,
get out.

Cross the bridge with missing slats,
run through the streets of my childhood,
go through the door to nowhere.
Take the suitcase
the house
the dreams
and don't forget the baby.

Nancy Jakobsson

Say Sean to Me

I know your names,

Sean, Andrew, Billy, Lisa, Mark,

Hannah, Sergio, Josh, Tara.

You were two, or six months, four hours,

five, nine, eighteen.

Your parents will never be the same,

your names written on their lives.

They will remember your birthdays,

the would have been,

measure the years by your friends.

Their dreams are unanswered questions.

They will sleep with your sweatshirt,

yearn for your scent.

Walk into your dark room

and hope you will be there.

They fear they may forget your face,

smile, voice.

And longing slips

into every corner of their lives.

They relive your last day, last touch,
but will it unravel their lives?

Your names entwine with my sons' names
my fears, my love for them.

And when time silences the voice of solace,
I will say Sean, Andrew, Billy, Mark,
Hannah, Sergio, Josh, Tara.

VI

Open Bowl, Two Handles

The Angle of My Repose

Pay close attention.

Notice the core.

Begin with a thin line,

then a broad stroke

curves to form the bottom.

Another angle to create the side,

then another.

Shade where it's dark.

Lift to find light.

Stand back and observe.

Core slants slightly left.

Left hip tilts out.

Right shoulder raised,

right arm extended,

the gesture of my subject.

Nancy Jakobsson

Closing Door

A door closing has a two-tone sound. The first is the push that we initiate.
The second is the door pulling itself in.

The sound of the front door closing
asks the question *what next*
as it pulls itself into place.
I slide the latch, metal on metal
my only answer.
It's just after a leaving
I am most alone.
Wait, come back, there's more.
The linger of want fills the space
like soft breath.
The thread of unsaid words
stretches taut and breaks.
I walk through the day
trying to close my fist on the missing.

Show Off

I don't like orange,
the color not the fruit.
I can get past color to eat one
but it's why I never liked Halloween-
pumpkins and candy corn.

Orange takes over sunsets.
Even in a bowl of fruit
it's in-your-face,
keeps the quiet banana
from the reverent pear.

Never mind it's the color worn
by humble monks and swamis.
I won't wear it.

I had an orange tablecloth.
I'd open the linen closet and
from its place among
solemn whites, holiday greens, pastels,
it shouted "me, me, me."

What relief
to place it in the Good Will bag.

Don't get me started on pink.

Nancy Jakobsson

It Happens

sometimes
on a Friday afternoon
In the middle of a session.
I disappear.
I quietly slide under the door
or hover near the ceiling. Someplace
where the words can't touch me.

No more sad stories for me,
I'm out of there,
drinking coffee in a small café,
or just waiting outside the door.

No one knows I've gone.
The understudy
knows all the lines,
the murmurs, the I sees.
She has perfected the body language,
slight forward lean,
steady gaze.

But she's cocky,
too sure of herself,
thinks she knows.
She gets in her own way.

That's when I slip back,
never missing a beat.
Until the next time.

Night Life

When darkness folds around
my sleeping self, books slide
from their upright postures.
By osmosis or diffusion,
ideas slip from pages,
into the stuff of my dreams,
an absurd observation from Billy Collins

Yalom infuses existential meaning
into every question. Thomas Wolfe
and Eckard Tolle pull the strings of soul.

Terry Tempest Williams counts
what's lost and gained.
Satire stages the family issues
and my photo album
supplies the cast of characters.

In the thin light of morning,
before dawn's gray light returns
a retreat begins back to the shelves
leaving only traces behind.

Nancy Jakobsson

When the Dead Come to Visit

Between sleep and light
when the dead come to visit,
they stop at the foot of your bed
search the dark for a lost memory,
told only in another sleep.
They brush your brow with
a touch light as old silk,
say your name in a familiar way.
Asking for nothing,
they bring an open bowl
with two handles,
forgiveness and assurance,
then recede on soft feet
into longing, a dark hall
where hours begin and end.

Dream Poem

Darkness flies above her head,

touches her hair with its wings.

No sound. The air

finds a place thats empty but for light.

Black becomes white, changes again

to blue and green,

becomes the astonishing world.